Black Ice

for my father, Denis Gartland Sullivan
(October 14, 1929—June 8, 2013)

i' vegno per menarvi a l'altra riva
ne le tenebre etterne, in caldo e 'n gelo.
        —Charon, Dante Alighieri's *Inferno*

(I come to carry you to the other shore,
to the eternal shades, to fire and ice.)

To Luke,
who know how to travel
over — and under — the black
ice of our lives.

Turning Point Books, Cincinnati

Published by Turning Point Books
P.O. Box 541106
Cincinnati, Ohio 45254-1106

Poetry Editor: Kevin Walzer
Business Editor: Lori Jareo

Visit us at www.turningpointbooks.com

ISBN: 9781625491541

LCCN: 2015950974

Cover and book design: David Allen Sullivan

Acknowledgments

Boxcar Review: Attending an Indian Concert
Caffeine Presse: Mask Making 101; 3 a.m. Fever;
      The Spring House
Enizagram: All Fall Down
Every Day Poems: The Last Game
The Fourth River: Flight
Hilltromper: Lost
I Am: Twenty-seven: Two Again.
Illuminations: Swimmer's Ear
Linden Avenue Literary Journal: I Want; Kronos
      Coughs Up His Kids; Reversals of Fortune
Missing Slate: Burn On
Phren-z: The Hang of It; What's a Father to Do?;
      Out of the Dark
Poetry Bomb: Outgoing Mail
PoetryMagazine.com: Life and Death Before Breakfast
Red Wheelbarrow: Drawing the Clock's Face; Earth Music;
      Morning Row, Swan's Island, Maine; Out to Pasture;
      Walking the Knoll; Waiting to Cross Lethe
River Styx: Palo Alto, California
Sliver of Stone: Wakey Wakey
Smartish Pace: Below Zero
Unlikely Stories: Scaling the Dream-Face; My Father's Face

Cover painting by Samantha Fields, *Leitmotif (Sequoia),* acrylic on paper, 11" X 11." Courtesy of *Western Project,* Los Angeles, CA, and *Traywick Contemporary,* Berkeley, CA.

I'm grateful to my poetry group who shepherded every poem towards completion and helped shape the whole: Chuck Atkinson, Barbara Bloom, Rosie King, Tilly Shaw, Debra Spencer, and Ken Weisner.

Thanks to the other poets and writers who critiqued these poems: Julia Alter, Len Anderson, John Arrant, Willis Barnstone, Ellen Bass, Sage Cohen, Susan Cohen, Kathryn DeLancellotti, Robert Fanning, Florence Fogelin, Rachel Hadas, Tina Kelley, Ann Kenniston, Danusha Laméris, George Lober, Roxanne McDonald, Adela Najarro, Robert Pesich, Frances Richey, Catherine Segurson, Roz Spafford, Eileen Sullivan, Brian Turner, Lindsey Wayland, and Al Young.

With deep appreciation for my mother, Margaret Henderson Sullivan, and my older brothers Kevin and Marc, for their willingness to let me write things the way I saw them, and for their unflappable love. Thanks to my father's friends and family who provided useful background information.

I'm blessed by my partner, Cherie Barkey, and my children Jules and Amina Barivan.

Contents

3. Enter the Fire

1. Daily Diminutions

This writing is especially important in brain damage cases because there's a lack of empathy between those who suffer and those who treat the brain-damaged.
      —from my father's accident recovery journal

      Our fathers
      carried us
      a long way into the world.
      They leave us one day, and die.
            And we carry them
            the rest of the way.
                  —Robert Sund

Black Ice I

My night train home was
delayed by snow and hard rain.
Dad waited, heat on,

as an aria
Cecilia Bartoli sang
bore him aloft.

I slapped the window
and he jumped, laughed. On Route Five
I told him Barbara

was breaking it off.
Knuckles whitened on the wheel
as I unspooled hurt.

*

Never saw that man
again. The next morning, still
comforter-cocooned,

heard: *Is he up yet?*
I'm going for the paper,
before he drove out

of our lives. Mother
and I were just sitting down
to bacon and eggs

when the hospital
called: *Your father's been in an*
accident. "How bad?"

Pictured him whistling
as car wheels grooved the slick road.
Come down now. Drive safe.

Darknesses

I'm afraid of attack. I'm not sure in what form
or when or why, but when I see the outdoors—
its shapes and sounds are those of attack.
  —from my father's accident recovery journal

Black on the windows, taped up
to prevent the men in Dad's head
from spying. Black on the windows
for the months his wife held him
when he balled up, cried, or *fuck-you'd*
the world. She believed he'd teach again,
relearn how to read and write. She
would be confidante and guide, her dream
of a PhD suspended. Her art books
bulged with slips of paper scrawled
with notes. She lived in darkness
until he was ready to tear paper down
for light that would blind them both.
She had gone with him on
the downward path—Virgil—
traveling as far as was permitted.

Drawing the Clock's Face

*His sports-related concussions and the car accident
predisposed him to frontal lobe dementia. What's
surprising is how he's been able to function and teach
with diminishing capabilities for these past twenty
years.*
　—Robert Santulli, M.D., Dartmouth Memory Clinic

I hear the doc's words
through a scrim of wanting Dad
to write it down right.

Numberless paper clock,
no hands but my father's, clenched
around a pencil.

Ordinal numbers
appear, half-drawn arrows fly—
then falter—erased.

My mother's ready
to accept diminution,
she's seen it daily.

Speaks of Dad in the
third person, a radio
she's learned to tune out.

While we talk he toils,
creating a patchwork of
fudged possibilities.

The doc turns to him,
What've we got here? Startled,
Dad finds our eyes. Stares.

Crosshatched palimpsest—
conflicting times of day traced
in ghostly overlays.

He hands it back with
apologies. *Couldn't find nine.*
The doc's all sugar,

sincerely thanks Dad
for doing his best. Both bend—
foreheads almost touch.

You've done fine, just fine.
He tacks the jittery clock
to a large cork board

and Dad sits straighter—
shy smile for his audience.
They shake hands goodbye.

Mom takes Dad's elbow,
guides him towards the flight of stairs.
Once there he shrugs her

off, looks hard at us:
You all go on without me.
I know you want to.

Back Home

Woodpecker's specialized skull
hammers out revelry
every goddamn day.
My near-deaf dad sleeps
through the racket, islanded.
He doesn't ask why I wake him,
folds me against his chest—
forty-odd years whispered away
as he strokes my hair.
His condition grows him kinder.
I've been wanting this without knowing it.
Mother's missiles are fistfuls of stones
hurled to put the bird to flight.
She curses as she launches each weight.

Judge

Even half here, Dad
whups us at Hearts without trying,
emptying all our

spades to pile on points.
Our astonishment amuses
him, and this, itself,

is a gift. He won't
remember, but he's here now,
big-bellied Buddha.

He holds Dr. Seuss
while my daughter turns pages.
Whispers his panic:

I can't read. We laugh.
"Neither can she. Make it up."
He wants yellow eggs…

He spills his coffee:
Goddamnfuckinsonofabitch!
Then smirks up at us.

I'm a lumbering
giant of over-cooked thoughts.
All I did, I did

under judging eyes—
but would he have disowned me
if I did dumb things?

Scrambled eggshell bits?
Put water in the crankcase?
Pulled the door marked *Push?*

Life and Death Before Breakfast

My mother edges out along the low stone wall
holding Mina's hand to show her the ripe
blueberries deer couldn't filch. I'm on the other
side when my mother slips and they're going over,
slow motion ballet where my mom folds arms
across chest—Pharaoh of falling—
rolling through the long grass beneath,
face calm. My girl pops up then kneels down
beside Grandma's form: *Are you alright?*
Let's do that again. My mom is fine,
but for a second she wasn't—
       her hip had shattered
       I was driving her to the hospital
       emptying her bedpan
       holding her hand
       kissing her
       goodbye...
              She picks up the bowl,
rejoins my daughter to recoup spilled fruit.

Touched

—Hood Museum, Dartmouth College

Dad and I visit
the mbulu ngulu
reliquary figures

that extend old ones'
sight, grant the living advice.
One enormous head

is a concave disk,
sparse features patterned from nails,
its reflective skin

touch-smoothed copper strips.
The young would sand-polish it
to see future loves

or the ones to fear.
We all want contact with worlds
that have gone before,

but this ancient head
the Kota carved is losing
luster behind ropes,

no skull at its base,
no ancestral bones beneath
to bless its magic.

My dad's hand rises
to stroke shimmery metal.
Panicked, I look round.

Gallery's empty.
Each sculpted elder aches to
have their features shined

by attentive hands
and the grit of sand—the gods
feel when we touch them.

Dad guides my palm to
the glint. *When you were young
your skin felt like this.*

The Hang of It

The mask my son carved: heavy warp of kiln-
hard clay, eye slits roughly gouged, edges

puckered where his fingers pushed through.
Nose, a pyramid, cut and sandwiched in two folds.

Diagonal, tractor-tire slash the only mouth.
A fright of dried hay sprouts from the top.

He takes it from me, gingerly, like some relic.
Stiffly bows to its hollow interior, eyes fill

holes as he raises his face to me,
a familiar foreigner. I say,

"Let's hang it up safe" pulling it off,
feeling the shell overfill my hands.

Earth Music

We hold hands to cross the jerry-rigged
bridge. Water-logged planks give beneath.

We unspool thin-skinned
Satsumas, then lie on sand.

My son places his head on my belly, points
where poplar leaves rise up in layers above us,

turning from dark green wind-tossed patches,
to speckled, to those seared by light.

We approach the creek, talk about surface
tension—I skim a flat oval stone.

He rises too, fists pebbles I know won't skim,
tosses them up instead. They rattle the creek.

It stops my arm to hear and I turn to watch.
Next, he flings a slew that ricochets off a log,

sends side-armed showers of sand that hiss-dance.
Then he has me toss in bass note boulders.

Open, heart, listen to liquid close over the largest:
One... Two... Three!

Attending an Indian Concert

I know her violin's
beyond him, but hope the man's
tabla resonates

in his diminished
world. He sees her bow bending:
Is she tuning up?

"Papa, you can't talk."
Why not? he bellows, *You are.*
Heads angrily turn

as Ramaswami
attacks a slow mangalam
and I find my way

to prayer. "Whatever
can mend this, let it come." Turn,
kiss his cheek. He calms.

He picks up my hand
and caresses it stiffly.
Music's in this touch.

We face front. Her bow
carves out the shape of sadness,
drum rounds pound my chest.

What's a Father to Do?

When my son fought me about getting in the bath—
clawing at doorways, denouncing me and all
the world's injustices—I clasped flailing limbs
to his sides and dumped him in the tub, fully clothed.
His mouth opened wide—
                              then he pulled me in.

Last Game

Dad won't follow suit
since he's playing Gin Rummy
while we're playing Hearts.

We take turns shouting
into his good ear. Each time
his turn comes around

he picks up a card.
When he fans out a flush hand
we call him the winner.

I replay the game,
convinced I can make him see.
These piecemeal goodbyes

hurt. Hard he'll never
shoot the moon, never chortle
when we gang up, lose.

I Want

to give my father
the whole crazy circus: clowns
in a tiny car

backfiring as they
lurch forward; choreographed
folly trumpeted

by the band; sweet reek
of sawdust soft underfoot;
family aerialists

defying physics.
I want him to be undone
by contortionists

pushing past body's
resistance, taffied. I want
him to ride the tent

earthward, show Bobo
her crate, blink back floodlights,
bark tear-down orders

through a megaphone.
I hand him the torn poster's
brash red bravado,

watch elephant tails
sashay bumps in unison
as the last truck leaves.

Kronos Coughs Up His Kids

In my mind I run
home movies backwards and laugh
at acts retracted.

I choose which to watch
and which to skip through. First time
Dad bellows *Quiet!*

a giant, inhaling
his cigar, his eyes bugged out
at dolls I unstack

along his desk's edge
and I hurtle backwards down
narrow attic stairs.

One night I feign sleep.
My father knows, but carries
me out to the car

and gentles me down.
Buckles my floppiness in.
Risks a wake-up kiss.

Pulls his lips from Mom,
unwraps her from him. I turn
the knob, door re-shuts.

A party unwinds,
as my Dad's colleague bristles:
America. You?

when asked: *Where you
from Nakamura?* Birthright of
an internment camp.

Next, we're at dinner
and I'm coughing up pellets
of peas, one by one

until my plate's full.
Then the light bulb assembles
itself and water

pings reentering
my squirt gun. Car's bumper
uncrumples, fishtails

backwards until straight
and racing from its headlights.
This time I say *yes*

when asked if I stole,
and slip the bills back into
his skin-soft wallet.

He walks backwards from
the tent where my wife and I
unmake love again.

And when he shoves me,
says I tripped him, I let him
spring up from the floor

to the hospital
gurney, swallow back curses
as the movie unspools.

Bed Down

I hanker after one groaning bed, that
four-poster, walnut-rich with geometric
sliced pineapple shapes surmounting
each lathed leg, and the curling
waves of the headboard pulling
in opposite directions.

It dominated my parent's bedroom,
the place I stole away to when left alone,
unearthing money caches
and sequestered chocolates,
the forbidding textures of bras and panties
and the astonishment of boxers.

I'd bring a slew of Mad magazines, or later,
an older brother's pilfered Playboys,
and like a dog I'd find that place
in the center where shot springs had sunk
to a stretched croissant shape—sweet
depression that fit my fetal form.

I'd read or masturbate or daydream
until a car door or *Anyone home?*
woke me,
and I'd flee the sanctuary
with a backward glance to check
I'd erased my presence.

I still see that dip this older body
might fit. I wonder
how they negotiated that ditch
between them, and whether
it was in the act of making me
that the metal sighed and sagged.

At Lou's Diner

Send a salami to your boy in the army.
        —Diner poster from the Korean War

Dad's pleased, looking up
from his cup of soup, saltines
he snaps in their wrap

before opening them.
Colorado's here, army
canteen where he found

soup the safest bet.
Pleased at cherry pies revolving
in their glass display,

red leaking onto crusts.
Pleased at meringues, strawberry-
rhubarb, and purplish...

balls? munitions? No,
wrong words. With effort he lets
the answer-search go,

lets them all slide by,
returns to minestrone,
breaks crackers apart

and lets them sift down
between thumb and forefinger,
grabs the word *pleasure.*

He spoons soup and crumbs.
Blueberries continue to wink
into view, reminding him

of what he once knew,
but the silverware's shiny
and the soup is hot.

Walking the Knoll

Oriole's reedy
outburst rattles the sunlight
into lumpen gold.

I nudge my father,
who pretends understanding—
can't hear a thing.

I see. He doesn't.
I've always wanted to catch
him out. Knew he didn't

know all he said
he did—it's my own habit
of bluffing when caught

short I want to nail
him with. The bird flutters on.
Music slips beneath

my wanting, the way
I'm astonished when my child
takes my hand in hers.

All Fall Down

I watch my father
fall, he grasps at the railing
that's telescoping

away, his feet scuff
each tread as his body turns
and looks back up

to where I'm stuck, lunging
for his hand—which seems to be
waving goodbye—

but just graze fingers,
miss the catch. He's laid out flat:
Get the hell away.

He never needed
anyone. That's what he claimed.
It was almost true.

I sit on the lowest
stair beside his prone body
waiting for sirens.

He doesn't want talk.
Allows me to lift his hand.
Holds onto silence.

Outgoing Mail

> *I have since learned—that is, since this morning—*
> *that my sons have found a guru who gives them the*
> *right spell for the right occasion.*
> —from my father's accident recovery journal

Email chains have linked
him to every internet scam—
Let me introduce

myself... Who could fall
for such obvious schemers?
Dad's protected well,

banned from bank accounts,
issued credit cards with barely
any credit. No

wonder he's feeling
powerless. For his own good
we assure ourselves

but constraints chafe him,
he wants to end-run them, give
his three sons something

more than he has left.
Now I've rerouted his mail
so it comes to me;

I read all he writes,
he's still suspicious enough
to couch his replies:

I will expedite
funds to you as soon as I
have reassurance

you will come through with
payment. Dad, your sons are well,
they have all they need.

Counting Change

From his bedroom comes
a crash: *Motherfuckingshit!*
By the time I'm there

the lampshade has burst
into flame and singed his hair.
I'm slapping at it,

he flinches, backs off.
His coin stacks fly as I beat
the burn down to smoke.

The bulb wears a crown
of brown plastic goo. I shake
the smoking shade: "Look,

you must've set it down
on the light after knocking
the support bar off."

He's incredulous.
Suspicious. Scared. *Don't know
how it got like that.*

When I hug him hard
he hugs me back. Forgiven
again, both of us.

In the Paint

Basketball slip-rolled
off my fingers as I jumped
above my father's

grasping hand, bank shot
kissed glass and glanced off the back
board of memory

to the wastebasket
of missed free throws and gym swears
where guys still play ball,

daring each other
to drive it past them. Father
falls away. I'm left

hanging, I've feinted
and now I'm past him, sending
the ball orbiting

above the rim—
I want the win, want him here
to face me again.

Mask Making 101

I lay down a smear of Vaseline over closed
eyes. My son's nostrils wrinkle at the smell.

To have Jules this still is an intimacy
rarely allowed now.

I drape plaster-soaked newsprint over
his features, mapping known mountains.

He disappears under headlines and blurred car crashes.
Feels like wet noodles, he says until his mouth's sealed

and only nostrils allow him to breathe. Strip
after strip builds him up, a hardening mirror.

Quietness discomforts me. I want him still to need
what I have to give. When he pulls it off

his double lies in his hands. He stares into it,
then turns it over. *Does this really look like me?*

I smile: "Just like you." *Your turn,* he grins back.
I lie down so his fingers can feather my face.

Coming Apart at the Seams

Bit by bit I take
apart my father's holey
rowboat that's been growing

petunias, circled
by flower-filled tire bumpers.
The brittle boards are

surprisingly spry.
I press boot sole to gunwale
and pull on the slats.

They splinter apart
in my hands. Discard pile mounts.
Paint layers revealed:

canary yellow,
fire red, filibuster blue—
tar and pitch traces.

*

At the summer house
on Swan's Island the last time
he can still visit.

I stare at his back,
framed by a rain-streaked window.
Dock's ring. Sailor's knot.

"What're you looking at?"
*Could have sworn I brought her up
on land but the rope's*

*headed straight on down.
Must have swamped her.* When I touch
his arm, he stiffens.

Evidence, piled up
against him, rises higher.
Here's another slat.

Long Distance

It's no good, he's gone,
my father shouts to my mom
after bellowing

at me through the phone.
He hasn't heard what I've said
but I feel closer

for hearing him breathe.
It must seem that others are
withdrawing from him,

the conspiracies
darkening, whispers contain
assassinations.

I think of floors built
to creak when the unsummoned
approached royalty.

I think of Father
roaming half-familiar rooms,
pricked by silences.

Her Heart Attack

Mom lies on the floor.
The man who loves her locked out
the ambulance men

who bang on the door.
He kneels and urges: *Don't let
them take you away.*

No time to lie down.
What is he imagining?
Who has she become?

He crouches, massages
her hand too hard, but her tears
confuse him. *Don't cry,*

I'll never leave you.
He already has. Dead bolt
gives way. They're kneeling

over her, checking
her vitals. Her husband's hands
frame her face. All fight

has fled his body.
He is staying with her, come
hell or high water.

2. Sons of Fathers

A raised eyebrow or a smile can acquire multiple functional significance in communicating reassurance, dominance, and/or subordination. We are always projecting masks of our intentions for others to read, though what they receive does not always match those intentions.
　　　—Denis Gartland Sullivan, *Happy Warriors: Leaders' Facial Displays*

　　Quand le père donne au fils,
　　rit le père, rit le fils;
　　El quand le fils donne au père,
　　pleure le père, pleure le fils.
　　　　—Jean-François Bladé, *Proverbes l'Armagnac*

　　(When a father gives to his son,
　　father and son laugh;
　　when a son gives to his father,
　　father and son cry.)

Black Ice II

My dad's hands were yanked
from the Datsun's steering wheel
as the bucket seat

back broke and he sailed
past racing telephone poles
and slurring pine trees

to shatter rear glass
and smash a pick-up's grille, then
drop back as the car

met the snowbank's fist.
His brain in its liquid case
slammed against bone,

contused as he stilled.
Back windshield diamonded him
in a blood-mask, streaked

by snowpack the dazed
truck driver used to stanch flow.
Radiator's shrill

broke through deadened ears.
We're thrown by what we don't know.
Ice slides beneath us.

Shaving Lather's Kiss

The bone-handled brush,
bristles all canted one way,
is hushed, then froths up

from the shaving cup
so dad can daub cottony clouds
on my puffed up cheeks

and play that his son—
five?—six?—is shaving. Heaven
is this heady smell,

the strop of the blade
singing wetly. He backhands
the unsharpened side,

pulls down airy clumps,
flicks them off baby-soft chin,
leaves a thin mustache,

dollops my pug nose.
Steamed mirror catches our ghosts
as they laugh and point.

He has not left yet.
He won't kiss me when he leaves.
I will not miss it.

His car idles in
the drive, white tail straightening
against winter's bite.

Nightwatch

Full moon, a cigar
burning a hole in the sky.
Silhouetted, Dad's

frame fills my doorway,
turns saliva-slicked leaves his lips
have kissed. He inhales

so the cheroot's eye
burns to make these quick sketches.
The designs he traced

still arc across my
retinas. Terse forms appear,
animals, my name

abracadabraed
in vanishing lettering,
and behind it all,

my father's bear-like
bulk, haloed by the hall light:
cyclops of goodnights.

3 a.m. Fever

I pick up the drum my son was playing
before sleep, lightly tap its head

as if its rhythm were a thread
that connects to his cycling breath,

connects me to all
who carry worn amulets

and chant down the gods
to comfort themselves.

I count breaths in sets of three,
gamble with blind gods:

"Please, make my son well."
I believe magic and prayers

can stave off our deaths for
a little while. I believe Jules hears

my breath, warm against his ear,
and that this drum head—thin

as skin pulsing at his temples—
calls him back.

The Spring House

Paint chips litter ground
around the fairy-tale hut
by the woods. Today

I accompany
Dad, who strips down to his trunks,
hands me the flashlight

and seal-slides into
the rock-walled well of chilly,
crystalline water.

I follow his moves
with the beam, chase whatever
he points towards. Weird light

throws his shadow selves
on the walls as he descends—
distends and distorts

his form as he grows
smaller than seems possible.
Frightened frogs leg off,

knobby snails dot rocks.
Three times he dives, hands feeling
for where water seeps in.

With his bend of wire
he reams at blockage until
spring's current strengthens.

Air bubbles balloon
up and burst on the surface.
He's from another

world. Bent legs launch him
towards me. He gasps, reaches for
the towel I hold.

Palo Alto, California

The littlest kids were all in bed, yellow trapezoids
of light spread on lawns held shadows of those
doing dishes. The pack owned these suburban streets
and I was running to join them
as they laid down rules for hide-and-seek.

I followed Carmen and her friend
but they hissed out: *Find your own spot, dork.*
I looked back, Fahd's forehead and arms
against the insect-crusted streetlight
seemed to hold it up. Meter of his counting ticked.

Behind fat bushes or in recycling bins, kids
were disappearing.
I'd already climbed the oak
once that day so it was easy to shimmy up the gutter pipe
of the flat-roofed shed and hide among its broad leaves.

Streetlights triggered on. I waited for their *ollieollieoxenfree.*
The full moon had cleared Critchlow's
by the time I climbed down and found them sharing
blankets and crude jokes. Flashlights played the trees.
No one had found me. No one had bothered to look.

Wakey Wakey

Five a.m. garbage run. I balance my coffee mug
in fingerless gloves. My compatriot in jolting

the neighborhood from sleep jerks a thumb
when the mechanism sticks and I descend to kick

the son-of-a-bitch into extending to grapple
another wheeled bin and bear it aloft. The bin

is beautiful against the blue-black sky—"Wait!" that's my son
inside, still pajamaed, shut in sleep,

and tumbling in with rinds and refuse.
I dive in, grab his disappearing ankle,

and yank him backwards, shouting to the driver—
but he's on auto-pilot, blind, oblivious—

next load's coming down, drowning us in everything
rotten or broken. Then I remember I hate the taste of coffee—

that oily black slick in the pot—when I was a kid
it meant Father was working again, couldn't be bothered . . .

Now my son's shouting for me from his bed, wanting what I
once wanted—hell—want still: to be keenly listened to.

I shake off coffee's mirage. Through the curtains' gap sun's
thermometer rises. I stumble towards my son and his dream.

Out of the Dark

I approach Nana's guest room—
haven't been here in years—
push open the door
and there's the rocking boy
on the pull-out day-bed
with its rough herringboned weave
of orange and black

just where I left him.
The grandfather clock
counts down its drip feed of hours.
Light gleams like whiskey
on a slurred tumbler.
Why were all the lights left on?
Who was taking care of him?

He's rocking hard, creak of the springs
must comfort. He shuckles like a Jew at prayer,
a flame dancing away from a wick,
unaware of me. His body oscillates fiercely
around some still center he can't reach.
My hand extends, stops just short
of his moving form. Do I dare touch him?

I bend to the rush of his breath,
see he's wearing my face
crosshatched by couch bruise,
that he's been waiting,
eyes clamped tight,
rocking through all these years.
I whisper: *Come, time to go.*

Summer at Cedar Ledges

The minor league rep saw me throw my fastball.
Ok, show me what else you got, *he said.*
That was the end of my baseball career.
—One of my father's favorite stories

Cumulus clouds roil
overhead—tops meringue-white,
undersides storm-browned.

I smell hot wet air.
The breeze riffles Lake Champlain.
My dad and I fling

flat stones, watch them ride
the surface tension, dimples
spread across wave-cheeks.

Dad leans down, sidearms
a baseball pitch that casually
nails every wave crest.

I try to mimic
his signature throw, desire
fixed to a stone's twist.

Boys Lounge After Swim, Lake Champlain

Marc bolted up, howling,
hand clenched on the angry bee,
fingers whitening

as muscles clamped down.
He knew he was allergic,
his arm would balloon

until it was useless,
so his hard fist was payback.
Dad pulled his fingers

apart, brushed wing bits
and furred body parts away.
Embedded stinger

he plucked between fingernails
and extracted. Marc didn't
resist, already

his palm was thicker,
whorls pushed out of proportion.
The scene rushes in

after Marc's divorce,
all those long years of regrets,
recriminations,

and the steely way
he brushed off all instructions:
"Let go Marc, it's dead."

First Death

I've just turned seven.
Some neighbors, seeking to take
down the ragged dogs

seen hunting the woods,
have set out a slab of meat
coated with strychnine.

Only our old dog
took the bait. We find her stiff
by the road. Dad's hands

lift her to the trunk.
I feel the weight, wonder why
he lays Sally there

instead of by me.
Want to clean her leaf-choked fur.
When I won't help dig

the hole, see her in
the ground, Dad pulls back, angry.
I bite the pillow

in my room. Look out,
the sack thwacks against his leg,
shouldered shovel shakes

every step he takes.
I watch until he parts
the close-packed branches

and they fall back.
I keep expecting to cry.
The green needled wall.

Pitcher

We slid a snail through the wiffle-bat's handle crack,
then my friend swung out to toboggan it down
to sloosh and end-smack into the bat's nose.
He'd dump out the mash and I'd choose a new recruit
whose shell would be split in turn. His mother
had approved of the genocide but hadn't sanctioned
such exuberance, the way his face heated up
as he crushed home runs. Those sickening smacks.
Nothing blots out the sound: me cheering him on.

Lost

I dog my father
uptrail at Mount Washington.
Mist swallows his form.

"Which way did he go?"
Scraggly pines shush me. I climb
a little further

thinking he'll wait up.
At the summit only wind whistles.
I conserve water

coming down. Pacing
by the car he kicks gravel.
What the hell happened?

Get in the damn car.
As I write this I now hear
the hard note of fear.

Bruised Paint

I see the ceiling spot
where the tennis ball dulled paint
centered above twin

beds in the room where
my brother Marc and I slept.
I hear the smudged spot

echo with our throws.
We lay on our backs and practiced
until we could chuck

even in the dark.
Catch and throw back. The dull whack
of words we unspooled

trying to understand
our Dad who'd driven to fetch
Marc from the police

station where they'd grilled
him for snitching Snickers bars.
He knew he was in

for it, gonna pay
big time. Then he threw the ball.
He spoke so softly.

Not one angry word.
Wanted to know how I felt.
I squeezed what I held.

Dad had other sides—
my brother was in the dark
as much as I was.

Below Zero

Tires scrawled cursive O's on the parking lot's expanse.
We were learning how to control a skid underneath
coned floodlights blurred by kicked-up flurries,
gravity's laws couldn't touch us. My father had done
this to teach me—now I was impressing Maria.
I cranked the wheel, she giggled, slid across
leather seats to me. We felt drunker than stolen liquor
could make us, spinning past Drivers' Ed. lessons.
We'd gone over the brink, skidded to a standstill, heads
still spinning, her lips locked with mine.
Later she claimed I'd kissed her, but it was
beyond us—something stopping wouldn't stop.

Stateside News During Dad's Sabbatical

—for Professor Jeffrey L. Pressman, 1944-1977

I woke to Father
shifting from foot to foot. Cold tiles.
He rubbed his eyes, crabbed:

Wie spät ist es jetzt?
to the black-corded phone. Mom
behind him, bit nails,

and hushed me harshly
when I asked who it could be.
His brusqueness softened.

I remember how
gently he reset the hook
into its cradle

before turning towards
her arms: *Jeff has killed himself.*
Took a hotel room

under a false name,
swallowed a handful of pills.
Couldn't keep them down.

Smashed through the window...
His hands shook loose midnight's air.
Then he broke, stumbled

towards her. He seemed
so small he would disappear.
She stroked his bald spot.

I pictured Pressman's
wild, comb-over, his pulsing

skin wreathed by cigar

clouds. Heard the quips
of Father's friends. Smelled brandy,
billows of laughter.

Men could kill themselves
even surrounded by love.
My father could cry.

Archduke Franz Ferdinand at
the Austrian Military Museum

Barely fourteen. My fingers smeared museum glass
as I traced the jagged lightning in the uniform—ink blot
I surmised was blood. The bullet bit through clothing
the seamstress had stitched him into that morning;
taut seams they didn't bother cutting, just knifed open
the fabric to lay bare his neck where an open hole
belched inarticulate blood. Franz Ferdinand's eyes
reflected faces of the uncomprehending. He asked
for his wife, his children, then burbled *Es ist nichts.*
I'd read the accounts but this was different, a man's
suit could jump the glass, lay gone hands on me.

Out to Pasture

How I loved that heap,
mounted on four cinder blocks
above front yard weeds while Dad
sprayed a new dent black,
shouting instructions from beneath the engine—
two-by-four propping the hood.
It was almost *mine*.
It had been through both my brothers—
one clipped a deer, so the hood was green
the rest rusty red—
except the tailgate, blue now,
since brother number two rammed a hydrant
that he claimed was totally
in a whacked-out place,
and did I mention the passenger door opened
every time you turned left so you had to haul
on the rope-lassoed handle to close it?
Or that the brown driver's seat
wouldn't stay up so you sat ramrod straight to steer?
But that was it, she was destined to be mine,
a father-shared project.

One day the school bus let me off with the creaking
of its hand-pull door and I saw the empty blocks.
"Mom, where the hell's my Datsun?"
voice a wild pitch.
Over the washer's clank she tossed back,
Sold for a buck to old man Dreyer.
I froze. "You did what?"
You always said it was junk. Got it off our hands.
It wasn't possible. That was just an expression.
"He'll return it, right? Once we explain . . ."
Nope, she clucked, *couldn't do that, it'd look peculiar.*
And that was the end.
He'd tightened the wheel lugs
and driven it off. All I had left were four blocks
and a rectangle of pale grass.

Test

After school we threw switchblades as close as we dared
to each other's shoes. Two circles of boys,
the four in play with legs splayed, and the hangers-ons
who talked trash or cast bets Rocchio would collect
and call. Girls, sometimes. Blades flickered awake
as we chanted and nailed throws that quivered the ground.
We'd toss at the foot to our right, then breathe—after.
The trick was to get close without piercing them
or flinching. The champions bled but shed no tears.

Two Girlfriends

One was a model citizen I could barely smooch.
Everyone wanted her, but no one dared force
Venus from her shell. No talk of the pill. On one date
I brushed her hair.
                    But the other girl
would meet me in the tower of stone on the hill
where carved initials shouted love, proclaimed
who'd fucked. I pushed her to do what I knew others
had done. We did everything but screw.
The tower was built as a fire lookout. Our desires
pressed against warm wood others' hands had worn,
and my flaming tongue licked at bare skin
that burned.
              Venus still demurred
when I insisted we go further. I was split.
Hated the one I'd entowered, who asked why
I wouldn't meet her anywhere else. I fingered
a singed heart in the wood,
                            struck a fresh match.

Two Again

I was a biter. It felt good to feel someone's flesh
between my teeth. And they'd come running,

pry me off, but the marks stuck: little O
of dents, sacrificial site.

They said I was bad. I feigned sadness, but knew
they were wrong. We make others ours

when we grip them tight—blood astonishments
mingled with their drier skin. Then I let them go.

Now biting's shared, takes us out
into the wilds where grass and moonlight

get at our skin. We play at the ragged edge
of desire, the animals in us loosed.

The Better Man

Dad showed my brothers
and me a way of wrestling,
feet splayed wide, rooted.

The goal was to move
the other off his mark, push
or pull him over.

We'd clasp opposed wrists
and crouch, each reading the face
of the other, fake

to see if we could
find weakness. Convinced ourselves:
This time I'll best him.

*

In Kurosawa's
Shichinin no Samurai
the master swordsman

is loath to murder
the less-skilled, who's been beaten
in the trial run

but doesn't know it.
The challenged master attempts
to rebuff the fool,

but when a push comes
to blows he unsmilingly
slices the man's neck,

all grimly serene.
Sword resheathed he turns away
before the man lands.

Stuck Holding the Ball

Kev and Dad play one-
on-one in the echoey
gym. Scuff of sneakers

and swears. They test
what the other's capable of.
Tied at ten, Kev fakes,

his fade-away clangs.
Dad muscles his eldest out
from under the rim.

My brother barks *Foul!*
Dad huffs and puffs about it,
then checks the ball off

Kev's foot. It rolls towards
the bleachers where I'm sitting.
Neither looks at me.

Locked in a stand-off
stare-down that stretches through years.
A janitor grunts

as he shuffles to
the control box and clicks off
thc lights, one by one.

Reading Faces

I'm reading his face
as I sift through these photos
the way he'd read ours

around the table,
calling out *zygomatic
ticks, quick smile onsets,*

mood incongruence...
In grad school he trained himself
on politicians,

watched video clips,
interrogated facades—
displays of power,

untended flinches
of fear—and here I am face
to face with a man

who withheld himself.
I reconstruct that truant
boy who was sent to

boarding school, who read
by flashlight in the closet,
who couldn't stand rules,

mocked authority
in all its guises, who ached
to be known and loved.

He counseled me once
to be careful, *You get hurt
too easy,* he said.

I now sense how fear
drove his PhD thesis,
the desire to know

more than others knew,
to see through *reassurance
displays* to hard truths.

*

And here I am, come
to place him inside these lines,
but he dances free,

jukes and jives, fullback
shucking off tacklers at Brown
until they threw him

out for not coming
to class. Only after years
as a lieutenant

did he return to grad
school. The grin he tosses back
in this portrait shot,

does it mean he wants
to be caught and cry? Or crack
the camera's ogling?

Morning Row, Swan's Island, Maine

Pulling backwards towards
his future, Dad hears oarlocks
click and catch each stroke,

feels salt spray lick him
from leeward and sights the shore
he is headed towards

by the house he's leaving.
With each oar dip he pulls it
smaller—pines swallow

up every window.
His eyes travel down broad blades
to where the oar swirls

tiny eddies, cupped
as if someone underneath
were holding them up.

He drifts, extends arms
that marry to the oars' wood.
His ribs are boat staves.

What was his back glides
on water. Nothing but sky
and wave slap, salt smack

and a flee of fish.
He's the water he's riding
and he's water's twin.

No destination
anymore, just this carrying
and being carried.

3. Enter the Fire

It's a good idea to have an empty head tonight. Almost all thoughts of consequences lead to worry and anxiety. The heart races, and you tend to mistake mental problems for physical ones. That long black cloud may not be outside the window at all.
     —from my father's accident recovery journal

Who would cry out
to the petals on the ground
to stay,
knowing as we must,
how the vivacity of what was *is married*
to the vitality of what will be?
    —Mary Oliver, *Lines Written in Days*
     of Growing Darkness

Black Ice III

*1. Desire to communicate but can't write (misuse of
letters), and can't talk (trachetraumatic)
2. There is a lack of taste and smell (depression)
3. Must eliminate distractions and emotional tensions
(mindful work)*
　　　　　—from my father's accident recovery journal

They wheeled a bloody
man who resembled my dad
past where I stood.

He rocked the gurney
so they had to strap him down,
rush him to surgery.

Through the swinging doors
I saw his bare feet dancing.
Then not. Then dancing.

*

Now we're home again,
in this place that's too well known,
encrusted by snow.

My father's eyes close,
he convulses my hand, breath
ragged as the window frost.

Assisted Living

My father wrestles
with the plastic ring sealing
the orange juice jug.

I want to tell him
how it works but resist, watch.
He presses it in,

but it doesn't give.
Lowers his glasses to have
a go at small print.

Takes a knife to slice
open the offending cap,
then reconsiders.

Again he bends low,
studies what obstructs desire.
This time his pinky

slips inside the ring,
dons the low-cost jewelry
that—with a jerk—breaks

free. He stares at it,
fills his glass, then balances
the hoop back in place.

Replaces the jug
in the fridge. He's not my son,
doesn't need my help.

¡Hay Caracoles!

Even getting lost
blesses, yields this nighttime square
shining in Seville.

Every table holds
steaming plates of buttered snails,
tiny shells like ears.

And every patron
wields a miniature forklet,
tears slippery meat,

slurps it past their lips
or uses it to punctuate
a salient point.

The dream's curt waiter
is a smallish man who bows,
ushers us to chairs—

rickety and frail—
asks what he can fetch for us.
We wave hands and point,

no one knows the word.
When he returns steam streams from
the uncovered dish.

With some practice we
get the hang of it—wine helps.
Parsley-flecked commas,

I can still taste them,
sliding down my throat like words
too smooth to master.

*

Clock reads 1 a.m.
Where am I again? I blink,
and my father leans

over the couch where
I'd been sleeping: *David?*
Where has Peggy gone?

I pat him calmer,
repeat Mom's itinerary,
then lead him to bed.

Wine-slick cobblestones
and butter fill my nostrils,
scent their apartment.

I rummage for words:
zeros? shell-case castanets?
Happily sleepless,

two places at once,
I marry mouth to hand to
folds of memory

undulating slow—
the way my father travels
these days, seamlessly.

Copy of Joachim Patinir's *Landscape with Saint Christopher*, 1520

*—for my father's student and our family friend,
Joost Van Nispen*

Joost left the bare in the guest room apartment in Barcelona
in memoriam. His lover, Antonio, had laid down the base
but hadn't finished detailing the faithful giant—over seven feet
by most accounts—before sickness made him leave off painting.

Mother stayed in the guest room with that canvas clamped
in its wood easel. She'd left her husband scuffing
slippered feet down too-bright halls, a child wearing diapers,
groaning wants. She'd carried him and all he carried.

Mother surveyed the canvas of whipped egg-white clouds above
a blue stream. Without figures it suggested what we'd all come to.
She saw the giant carrying the Christ child on his shoulder,
imagined his complaints as he soldiered on, the water stacking up

against thighs, past waist, heaving chest,
the child's pudgy finger pointing the way gleefully.
She knew that when he set down the child
he found himself blessed by a weight released.

Waiting to Cross Lethe

Fake bus stop was made
for memory-loss patients
so they'd have a place

to wander to. There
they sit in a row, waiting
for the forty-six

that doesn't exist.
My father studiously
takes me there to show

he's living it up.
Driver of the shuttle bus
comes on the hour,

reassures them this
is the one they're waiting for
and takes us around

the block and back to
the wing where the bars that frame
the yard are hidden

within high hedges.
*There, you see? Takes a little
initiative, but*

it's a lovely trip.
And with what deference José
takes each patient's arm,

asks how they liked it,
listens as if he's never
heard their words before.

Appetites

As I feel better the sun shines more brightly and as
I see the sun I walk as close as I can towards it.
                    —from my father's accident recovery journal

We wheel our father
out of the dementia ward
through pass-code-barred doors.

His head lolls forward,
triples his chin, and his eyes
are recessed, piggish.

He shouts *giddiup*
to speed my older brother
who motors him on,

waves fatted fingers
towards where he wants to travel.
We give him choices

only when we're sure
what he'll choose. He takes us
outside, sucks up air.

I pluck a birch leaf
for him to feel. He sniffs once,
turns it over, then

pops it in his mouth.
I squeeze his cheeks to pry out
the pulp as he claws

my hands and complains,
gagging on stringy veins: *Mine!*
"Marc, please don't tell Mom,

she'll go ballistic,
say I poisoned him." I chew
in camaraderie.

It's tart, astringent.
He points at another. We could
feed him the whole tree.

Reversals of Fortune

My father had suffered reverses in business from
1929-1935 and eventually died of a heart stroke. He
was often ill and hallucinated at night. I remember
very little of this period except isolated instances. For
example, I recall vividly coming downstairs one ni
 —[sic] from my father's accident recovery journal

Dad wet his bed too,
though he phrased it softer:
Your grampa helped me

when I had troubles
in the night. Removed wet sheets,
rocked him in sleep's well.

The one memory
Dad held after grampa died
before Dad turned ten.

Night kindness rendered
half-blind by a sleep-deprived
man whose cigarette-

saturated skin
was an October of leaves.
The way my grampa

would stroke my dad's back.
I want to own Dad's small ears,
hear Grampa's bass-notes

beside my father's.
I want to hear the bad heart
that would confine Gramps

to bed—where he'd rail
at those who'd failed him—demand
what he couldn't reach.

I hold what my dad
held onto, a hand slipping
free from his fingers,

a tenderness that
still burns—a night light's frail note
as the door clicks shut.

Scaling the Dream-Face

> *Dear David,*
> *Thank you for your message. I will be too happy to see*
> *you here. And I would love to come out to California to*
> *visit you and your family there.*
> *Love, Dad*
> —my father's last email

The dream has me back
home. I lie sodden newspaper
over his still face

to create a death
mask I barely recognize
as familiar.

The house-high forehead,
a skew of nose, blown back hair
like stubborn sea grass—

whitened, retreating—
double chin that threatens to
triple, smirk of lips.

There seems to be more
of him than I remember.
I'm close to the end,

and the spongy soup
of plaster-of-Paris swirls
in the plastic bowl.

As the last slap seals
his stoppered mouth a burble
distends smeary words

and his sunken chest
rises high. "What the...?" Claw up
what I've created,

pull apart thin shells
of gluey plaster and yes,
put my lips to his,

seal my open mouth
to one I have to pry open,
force hot air into.

Then cross palms and press
just below his sternum, hard.
Watch his face. Nothing.

*

I stop shaking him.
Retrieve shreds of wet newsprint
from the floor, refit

casts to their places.
Begin again to cover
him. Body lies there

while I do my work.
Plaster sucks all the moisture
from my molding hands.

What if Gods are *Less* Than Us, Not *More?*

What if they're blessed with attentiveness,
an unceasing *yes* they mound on life like butter?
They never grow up, never grow older, never

cease their open-mouthed astonished nodding.
They're witnesses we long for even when alone,
ears that never close. We pour in what's worst in us;

they gargle poisons. Greedy beggars dying to try
every blesséd thing, and promptly forget what they've tasted.
Like my dad, whose circular greetings could go on

all day. His condition means he never tires of seeing
my face near his own, pulls me to his coarse cheek,
tenderness surprises. One more good greeting.

My tears come from remembering who he was,
his come from remembering who I am. It won't last,
but in this moment he's a child of the gods.

My Father's Face

In this print from 1887, the Dartmouth Inn wears
a blotchy skin. I only know it's fire by the caption.

Hoses carve across white snow. Men hold a black serpent
from which an arc intersects the white of the flame.

In this photo they're the same, fire and water
reduced to smeary chemical traces. White sky fills

glassless windows where one wall still stands.
Carriage on runners—the horse probably unhitched

while skittish with fear—trails black spaghetti reins.
In the foreground a silhouette suggests a man,

hands deep in his pockets, watching the disturbance,
as I do, from a safe distance.

Mirror Mirror

Father's face appears
in my mirror, grey hairs march
backwards from the prow,

obeying commands
from some other ship's captain,
mutinous eyebrows

white as dead coral.
Pug nose I'd seen broken, healed.
My brothers' faces

rise up inside me
like angry fish. What we shared
was a family line,

but this is different.
He doesn't soften his gaze
with easy laughter,

he only stares back
as intently as I stare.
Suddenly I see

through him to men
who'd sing down Irish shanties
between whiskey shots,

who'd curse the wayward
sheep that made their supper cold,
take it out on wives.

I see great-grandfather
board the freighter in Canada
as a winch man, then

disappear dockside
in Chicago to see what
he'll make of himself

with his forged papers
and a copper of pluck and
determination.

I see the one-eyed chief
who first took O'Sullivan
as his nom-de-plume.

Behind him, nameless
men come shouldering forward
to crowd my mirror.

Enter the Fire

I have resisted
direct address, as if nearness
could embarrass you.

What would it have cost
to reveal what harried you?
Whatever heat you

ran from I run to,
as if the house were on fire
and I broke your grasp

to grab what you left.
Dementia lowered your guard,
made you speak secrets.

*

One of the stories:
seduced by a relative,
but the family

laid the blame on you,
just kicked out of Brown. Sent to
a shrink, then drafted.

All sexuality
became suffering, bottle
rocket pocketed,

until your lover
shared her history, became
your conspirator

and wife. But we three
sons are drawn to that fiery
blaze you kept at arm's

distance. Passionate,
awkward lovers of women,
discomforted by

our animal lusts.
But I *will* be comforted
by you, even now.

*

My mirror holds you
in its circumscribed framing.
I yearn to know you,

and through you, know me.
You are everywhere I go,
reluctant shadow

rising to greet me.
You've been where I'm traveling.
You are the roadbed

and the map, the burnt
cloud clap of first rain that stings
in its sideways yaw.

But I remember
how you confessed amazement
at the way I live

light and travel hard—
at this strong woman I chose.
You took me this far,

now I'm looking back
at your waving, blurry image
through a scrim of flame.

Flight

The day Dad's felled by a stroke
from which he won't recover, I bike
my daughter to school as always.
High on a telephone wire
a speckled hawk-back—
plumage roughed against
the cold—is perched. Red-tail turns,
looks through me as always. This time
I drop my bike, raise my cell phone
to take a photo. The screen shows only
arcs of the quivering wire.
No one's called me yet.

Losing My Touch

My mother likes her,
Dad's favorite nurse, who helps
us reposition

his grumbling bulk.
He still attracts sexy help.
She hugs Mom tightly,

soothes down anxious hairs.
Mom stifles cries, then pulls back,
apologizes,

kisses just my brow,
and leaves. The nurse fetches ice
and a plastic spoon.

I have her show me
how to slip chips in. I'm flirting
past his stroke-stilled form.

Tears well, blur her shape,
but I will them on hoping
she'll comfort someone

whose world's imploding
like a star. I lay my head
where she can reach it.

Birth

Let me take you to
the room where death's being born.
Even attending

nurses grow quiet
slipping free the warm bed pan,
rolling his whale-bulk

to change sweat-soaked sheets.
See how his earlobes are creased?
They always do that,

says the nurse. As if
some angel were pinching them.
They've re-settled him

on half the raised bed
so I can snuggle in, drape his
unresponsive arm

over myself, child
in. My father's dying. Ice
sweats the plastic cup.

Digging in Black Mountain, New Mexico

They decorated the interiors of the bowls, which
were upended on the deceased's head and "killed"
with a sharp object. The resultant hole in the vessel
presumably allowed the spirit to escape.
     —J. J. Brody, *To Touch the Past:*
         Painted Pottery of the Mimbres

I shape the bowl, coil
crimped to coil, working outward
until it's the size

of his skull. It's formed
in the style of the Mimbre—
a snake soothed with slip—

but no elder holds
my hands, just these photographs
to guide my shaping.

Before it's entombed
in the kiln I paint inside
a rectangular

man, big eyes and grin,
chortling over some joke,
arms trailing feathers.

My dad's still alive,
but the spirits of his pasts
circle closer than

his own family.
I imagine his spirit's flown,
that I'm alone with

his body. I place
the bowl over his thin flag
of white hair and strike…

*

I step out, look up
into the black bowl of night,
patterned by piercings.

Beached

The room is half dark.
Arvo Pårt's strings sigh the air.
Kev sits on one side

of his heaving chest,
me on the other. The shaking
of his death rattle

has become part of
the music that stills the room.
I read a poem.

Kev lowers one hand
to the laboring heart and says:
Go if you want to,

stay if you need to.
Ocean swell lifts, a red wave
rises through neck and

face, suffuses him
with color and a last breath
he releases. Blanched,

the sea draws away
and leaves his body to our care.
A weight to be held,

washed clean, and hoisted.
In a few days it will be burned
down to nubs of sand.

Burn On

My brothers and I
lift our dad's bier, carry
it to Lake Erie

where he rode freighters,
mastered jibs, the luff of sails,
outdid his brothers

in half-assed races
that terrorized lesser craft.
He rests on crossed sticks.

In the dream it takes
all three of us to keep it
from tipping. Shoulders

drop it to the boat
that squelches lower, freighted.
Marc thumbs his lighter,

shields flame with cupped hand.
We shove the dinghy away.
If the chop sinks it

so be it. Wave slaps
knock it about, but it's true.
What music led him

to stand at the back
of the Protestant chapel
perched on Swan's Island

in his last free years?
Dad, who mocked religion,
heard something singing.

What prayers should we leave
as he turns to fiery ash?
A last *bon voyage?*

Mother Says: *He'd Want You to Have It*

Sweater becomes me, like Hercules' gifted robe.
Bites at my skin, raw Irish wool. Can't stand
to be so close. It grambles on in my father's voice
of hard work. I manage, after many washings,
to wear it with a turtleneck so I don't have to suffer
direct touch. I don't know what they call this
interlaced diamond pattern, enough that it stays,
folded in my drawer, until the days become
cold enough to don second layers.

Cathedral

—for Walter Holtkamp, Holtkamp Organ Company

The construction crew's 6 a.m. nailgun
shoots apart my sleep while hammers
pound in daylight's headachy glare.
Someone's erecting a dream next door.

I put in earplugs from my nightstand and
stumble towards the shower only to find
every sound's attenuated, water plays
a whole new set of scales. I dance
and shake as a jackhammer rattles.
The towel whispers like sandpaper.

I flick on the electric shaver I took
when cleaning out my father's effects
and attend to a thrum running around
and through my head as if I were a cathedral.

In my twenties I hitchhiked to Belgium
to meet up with Dad's friend
from boarding school days. Walter
led me to a church so he could try
the just-installed organ. How I spun
through the forest of stony pillars
like a low-ranking dervish of desire
as he played the furthest pluck points.

Now I spin inside my skull to the back-
beat of construction tools, the clear *chiff*
of rebar rattling against rebar,
backhoe's pedal boards being depressed...

Once I caught my father intoning an off-
key aria with headphones clamped
around failing ears. He spun inside
his private paradise, which I got to share
until he caught my shadow.

Ashes, One Year Later

My brothers and I
throw Dad from the knoll's summit.
He showers the leaves.

Small particulates,
wind-lifted, rise and burnish the air:
Vesuvian dust

silting eyes, eddies
dancing currents, whisked remains
of his ash-grey hair.

How little we know
of the wayward upper airs,
their ways of going.

I lick dusty bits
from fingers—powdery talc
on a gymnast's hands.

On My Knees

The slug-like comma of shampoo
slurps into my palm—hair already wet.
My family's somewhere in the house,
their voices tinned. I sit on the tiles,
stare at the drip-pocked comet
as if it's the entrails of some animal
that holds answers to my future.
I rub palms until shampoo lathers,
draw designs on my body. *He is in me...*
I will a spirit to descend on ropes of
water, to feel touched by some Other.

I see my father, his body
at the other end of being,
bloated, beached on the hospital bed
in that darkened room, hear guttery
ragged breaths through the good half
of his mouth that will not swallow
food or water anymore. I see us
together in the locker room showers,
the way he unselfconsciously soaps
his ass and cock, the graying armpit hairs,
how his comfort discomforts.

A knock. *You ok in there?* Tears
well even as I speak reassurances
and stand to wash away the whorls
I've made through body hair.
I close eyes to feel the shampoo
and my legs splay on washed-off excess—
arms pinwheel as I catch
the shower curtain, which gives
way with the *pup-pup-pup-pup*
of grommets until I'm down on all
fours, laughing for all I'm worth.

Status Update

My dead father friended me on Facebook
today. I recognized his grinning mug
since I'm the one who uploaded that look,
minus my mom. Algorithims trigger
such messages, I'm aware of that fact,
yet still I felt a little uptick in
my heart, a strange elation that he cracked
the code to invade my computer screen,
reaching out to me as he so seldom
did while with me. *Spíritus Sáncti. Amen.*
He teases me with that devilish grin,
is this another lesson in lessening?
I hit *confirm.* And send him a reply:
Are you freed from the living when you die?

No End

—at Labrang Monastery, Tibet

Dad, what have I done
with you? Like slain Osiris
whose body was strewn

up and down the Nile
only to be rooted out,
you've been scattered:

turn up in photos,
in mirrors, Jules' anger,
words I've chiseled at

divide us in two.
I would kiss you and kill you,
tell a rebirth myth

in which the pieces
cohere, recreate myself
outside the story

you started in me.
Every field I walk's littered
with words you planted.

You read my first poem,
said: *You loved her, didn't you?*
and it became true.

*

I tear you into
bits, like printed paper prayers
the Tibetans throw

to the winds. Colored
shreds that bleed into the earth,
travel down ravines

with seasonal rains.
I watch monks cut apart monks
who have died. Scatter

vulture packs with strewn
body parts. They believe it
will cure attachment,

teach how body bags
are unwieldy vehicles
for what carries us.

Swimmer's Ear

Do the dead still dream?
Do burning waters they crossed
still crease their pupils?

Do they hear the tick
of children's clipped fingernails
as scissor halves meet?

Do their hands grasp oars
that have rotted into punk?
Are their dreams ours?

Maybe it's our dreams
of them that keep them breathing,
shallowly, our ears

haunted by their death-
rattles that never expire? They're here.
They hop on one leg

like swimmers trying
to shake loose that drowned feeling,
the way my father

hammered on one side
of his head after a swim.
Water gushes out

the world surges in.

The author and his father

David Allen Sullivan was born in Champaign Urbana, Illinois, where his father was earning a doctorate. After a year in Palo Alto, David spent most of his childhood in Vermont, while his father taught Political Science at nearby Dartmouth College, conducted research on politicians' facial gestures, and took the family on a one-year sabbatical in Vienna. David attended the University of Chicago, and went on to study with James McMichael at the University of California, Irvine, where he earned his PhD. His first book was *Strong-Armed Angels,* and three of its poems were read by Garrison Keillor on The Writer's Almanac. *Every Seed of the Pomegranate,* a multi-voiced series of poems about the U.S. invasion of Iraq, followed. With Abbas Kadim he co-translated the selected poems of Iraqi Adnan Al-Sayegh, which was published as *Bombs Have Not Breakfasted Yet.* David teaches at Cabrillo Community College, where he edits the *Porter Gulch Review* with his students, and lives in Santa Cruz with his love, the historian Cherie Barkey, and their two children, Jules and Amina Barivan. He was awarded a Fulbright, and taught in Xi'an, China for one year: yesdasullivan.tumblr.com. His poems and books can be found at http://davidallensullivan.weebly.com/index.html

CPSIA information can be obtained
at www.ICGtesting.com
Printed in the USA
FSOW01n0537230915
11416FS